W9-ADX-809

HOUSE *of* DAYS

HOUSE
of
DAYS

POEMS BY

Jay Parini

❧

Henry Holt and Company

New York

Henry Holt and Company, Inc.
Publishers since 1866
115 West 18th Street
New York, New York 10011

Henry Holt® is a registered trademark of
Henry Holt and Company, Inc.

Published in Canada by Fitzhenry & Whiteside Ltd.
195 Allstate Parkway, Markham, Ontario L3R 4T8

Library of Congress Cataloging-in-Publication Data
Parini, Jay.
House of days : poems / Jay Parini.—1st ed.
p.   cm.
ISBN 0-8050-5713-7 (alk. paper)
I. Title.
PS3566.A65H68   1998   97-28897
811'.54—dc21

Henry Holt books are available for special
promotions and premiums. For details contact:
Director, Special Markets.

First Edition 1998

Designed by Michelle McMillian

Printed in the United States of America
All first editions are printed on acid-free paper.∞

1 3 5 7 9 10 8 6 4 2

Acknowledgments are due to the editors of the following magazines,
where many of these poems first appeared: *Boston Review, Kenyon Review,
Poetry, The New Yorker, Ontario Review, Oxford Poetry, P.N. Review, Sewanee
Review, Southern Florida Review, Tar River Poetry, The Yale Review, Verse,
William and Mary Review.* "Some Compensation" first appeared in *Poems
for a Small Planet: Contemporary American Nature Poetry.*

The symbol •   •   • is used to indicate a space between stanzas of a
poem whenever such spaces have been lost in pagination.

For Devon,

without whom I would rather say nothing

ARS POETICA

A swallow flickers past my eye:
this bird whose name will never follow it
to where it sleeps,
or save its feathers from the dust of time.

CONTENTS

I

Nature Revisited

STARS FALLING

Fire-flakes, flints: the same old stars
still fiery in the unredemptive sky,
the silvery and hopeless midnight sky
that feels like home from here to Mars,
then gradually grows foreign into stars
we hardly recognize, that fill the eye
with lofty gleanings we ineptly scry
by framing legends of unending wars.

There is some comfort in the way they sprawl,
their vast composure in the cold and careless
spaces that absorb them as they fall,
their dwindling into dark with less and less
of anything a witness might recall,
the ease of their becoming homelessness.

SWIMMING AFTER THOUGHTS

In memory of Robert Penn Warren

Across the blackened pond and back again,
he's swimming in an ether all his own;

lap after lap, he finds the groove
no champion of motion would approve,

since time and distance hardly cross his mind
except as something someone else might find

of interest. He swims and turns, eeking
his way through frogspawn, lily pads, and shaking

reeds, a slow and lofty lolling stroke
that cunningly preserves what's left to stoke

his engines further, like a steamwheel plunging
through its loop of light. He knows that lunging

only breaks the arc of his full reach.
He pulls the long, slow oar of speech,

addressing camber-backed and copper fish;
the minnows darken like ungathered wishes,

flash and fade—ideas in a haze of hopes
ungathered into syntax, sounding tropes.

•   •   •

The waterbugs pluck circles round his ears
while, overhead, a black hawk veers

to reappraise his slithering neck, and frogs
take sides on what or who he is: a log

or lanky, milk-white beast. He goes on swimming,
trolling in the green-dark glistening

silence and subtending mud where things
begin, where thoughts amass in broken rings

and surface, break to light, the brokered sound
of lost beginnings: fished for, found.

RAIN BEFORE NIGHTFALL

Late August, and the long soft hills
are wet with light:
a silken dusk, with shifting thunder
in the middle distance. Chills
of fall have not yet quite
brought everything to ruin.
And I stop to look, to listen
under eaves. The yellow rain
slides down the lawn,
it feathers through the pine,
makes lilacs glisten,
all the waxy leaves. The air
is almost fit for drinking,
and my heart is drenched,
my thirst for something
more than I can see
is briefly quenched.

AT BARTLETT FALLS

As if from nowhere:
moss-green water
gathers to a knot, then frays,
a trembling of white foam,
then black-on-black collecting in a rockpool,
trickling through a weed-scrim,
disappearing.

Soul is like this.
It astounds with presence, sweeping
to a veil of raveled beauty.
You can pass your hand through its fine spray,
its rainbow aura:
fractionated, fresh. The air
is ionized around
its glitter-fall in place.
And then the trickle
into rushes, fading hiss,
the soft dispersal into soppy ground.

THE LAKE HOUSE IN AUTUMN

There's silence in the house at summer's wake.
The last leaves fall in one night's wind,
the mice are eaten, and the cats begin
a rumbling sleep. There's nothing much at stake.
It's not quite cold enough to stoke
the furnace, and the neighbors never seem to mind
if leaves are raked. I'm staring through a blind
at less and less beside a cooling lake.

I keep forgetting that this absence, too,
must be imagined. What is still unknown
is still beyond me, as with you.
The mind is darker, deeper than a windblown
lake that tries to mirror every hue
of feeling as the season takes me down.

WILLOW SONG

Willow willow, drooping gold,
there is a story you have told
of how you cast your locks upon
a cold stream always passing on.
Your melancholic, bold display
is just the gesture to appall
the trees beside you standing tall
and primly saying nothing much.
They hate the way you seem to gush,
as if relief were to be found
in falling forward to the ground.
It makes them wince to see you bend;
they're wondering what you intend.
Your grief in gaudy limbs unfurled
like garments rent before the world
is just too much for them to take.
(They think, in fact, it's all a fake.)
But willow willow, I'm with you.
If only I could cast my rue
in similarly lush cascades
of desperate, abandoned braids.

SOME COMPENSATION

Trees in the forest fall and, falling, find
some compensation in the way they fail.
The mites become them, riddling the bark
that loosens slowly over many summers
as the fog surrounds and seeps inside.
A punky softness is the telltale sign
that what was once so thoroughly contained
in lines of strict and vertical composure
has begun to let itself convert
to earth and water, air and maybe fire:
combustible, a decomposing mass
where energy converts itself again
from this to that, shape-shifting spirit—
protean and pure in each new guise.
So pocks are filled with exoskeletons
and digging legs, with flywings, dust of eggs
that hatch and swarm; a nest is broken
and becomes a teeming, homely city
where a worm may sleep and fall to slush;
where what was wood is turned to gases
that will heal the sky; where tubers feed,
the tiny shoots emerging, gaining into green,
absorbing water that has been contained
in spongy pulp, in moss that covers
with assuaging fur the log's bare skin.
What a feast is made of what has fallen
and the wind, as patient now as ever,
circles and assumes this shape or that one,

always moving on: from leaf to lizard,
seed to finch to splatter in the mud,
where breath begins, where eyes fall open,
where the world invents itself again.

THE DISCIPLINE OF SEEING

How can I begin to say what's here?
In north New Hampshire woods turn rough
with jackpine, scrub oak, thistle;
granite edges flake in sunlight,
and the dirt is sandy, roots
like old hands swelling at the knuckles.
Air is whiter, lakes are bluer:
pieces of old sky that fell to earth.
The wind seems far too high today
as white pines rustle at enormous height,
a lofty, lush, deep-throated whir;
its broad effects are all on view,
if only you can train the eye to watch,
to focus properly on what presents
itself in time, in taste and color,
shapes that shift from hill to valley
and demand continuous transcription.
It is always difficult to hold,
to place a moving landscape in the mind,
where language feeds upon the given world.

A KILLING FROST

Beside the pond in late November,
I'm alone again
as apples drop in chilly woods
and crows pull tendons like new rubber
from a roadkill mass.

Ice begins to knit along the ground,
a bandage on the summer's wounds.
I touch the plait
of straw and leafmold, lingering to smell
the sweet cold crust.

An early moon is lost
in sheer reflection,
wandering, aloof and thinly clad,
its eye a squint of expectation.

I know that way,
this looking for a place to land
where nothing gives,
these boundaries of frost and bone.

AFTER DARK IN TUCKER'S WOOD

I go a long way out
as dark climbs down the staircase of each tree,
and tongues begin to wag.

So much is going on that nobody will know:
the owl's devouring dive to feed,
its hairball vomit,
coydogs wailing through an open field
in fool pursuit of yellow moonlight,
rodents mating on a dump
and, soft, nearby, a buck's despair
in late November as it curls to sleep.
I can't think why
the sun must rise to validate a story.

Now I linger at the edge of town
if only for a glimpse of what I'm missing
as the night hoods over.
I would like to know what happens when you sleep,
what tales are fetched from Tucker's deep.

WHO OWNS THE LAND?

Who owns the land?

Not I, the sparrow.
I have seen it passing, and have dropped
to taste its lively worms. I've built a nest
in its red oak and fluttered in the sky
among my children as they learned to fly
above the field. We all have fed here.
Many of us died: so many feathers,
dust of wings.

Who owns the land?

Not I, the fox.
I merely hunt among its shadows.
In the land of snow, I leave my tracks.
In summer corn I pick my way.
I dig my holes, but I owe nothing
to the bank of fools. I borrow time.
I burrow and I bend to every season.
I will come and go, like you—and you.

Who owns the land?

Not I, the frog.
Even though I take my coloration
from the land I wear, that wears me out.
I merely swallow what the air provides:

a thousand wings, good taste of fly.
I'm hardly more than mud myself,
and nobody owns me.

Who owns the land?

Not I, not I.
I simply live here. Here I die.

NATURE REVISITED

A sparrow hawk has swooped,
a field mouse failed behind the Kmart
in the empty lot where dandelions sprout
in blacktop cracks.

The sun's gold kite is flying overhead,
monotonously high;
heat hangs like someone's bright idea
gone awry.

Hello, it's summer,
and the world is full of fiberoptics.
Everyone's on-line, their e-mail begging
for a rapid answer.

Mothers with their pudgy, fevered children
wait in corridors, in plastic chairs.
The intercom is talkative today.
The mothers pray

as fish are drying in the local stream,
and billboards shimmer.
Tarboils pop in fresh-laid roads
as cars slur by.

There's new construction going on quite near:
white glass and cinder block and steel.

The trucks like yellowjackets buzz;
they sting and disappear.

The sky is falling, piece by piece,
like weakened plaster.
It is hard to find the wilder world,
what nature was.

Look in thickets of a thousand sorrows,
under bridges or behind the malls,
in hedgerows leading nowhere in the dust,
or over walls

for what is missing. It is there.
You'll see.
Hello, it's summer.
It is there. You'll see.

II

House of Days

HOUSE OF DAYS

1. JANUARY

The red fox picks its way.
It roots in gullies
for a nesting vole, a field mouse
stranded by the freeze.

All night the attic teemed with mice
like unformed thoughts,
their small feet crumbling through a thousand pages
of the boxed-up books I've never read.

The children are asleep,
their shallow breaths the rise and fall
of generations, though I know that winter
will consume them, fix their thoughts
(like mine this morning) on the only end,
when what is passing has been passed,
unhoused at last.

I look up from my desk:
the glassy light is hard to see through,
slantwise, chill.
The old white house grows whiter still.

There's silence in the sheets
that gather on my desk,
and I want to read somewhere of something

that is not this empty winter wait
for what will happen
in the wake of colder things to come.

2. FEBRUARY

A lace is spread
against the high black table of the night.

I'm walking in an orchard near my house
as stars detach and flutter into air.

The apple trees are bare,
but flakes are heaped like sugar on their limbs.

The roads are drifting deep with stars,
the ditches filling,

and the house dissolves—
the clapboards fading white on white.

In a blink, it's gone:
the life I knew,

till sweeping winds invent a syntax
I may try to use

to re-create my house,
its soft, bright lines,

•   •   •

floor after floor, the stanzas
rising through a snowy gauze,

the chimney poking through a scrim
of powder into hard, black time.

3. MARCH

The sun is cold and yellow
on my study wall.
I nose among the books,
those written and unwritten,
dust of thought that clings or passes.

Love that's come and gone
means less now,
though I wish I'd known when I was younger
that a simple phrase can last forever,
if it's only true.

Beyond my window, in the snowy field,
the sun has found reflected glory
I could never match.
I let that light fall on my page.

The way of silence is a lasting way,
a darker way,
but not this month this mood this matter
that I waste my heart on,
web of words, this still-becoming
text that's spun to catch whatever falls.

4. APRIL

The ice-floes shelve in alabaster streams,
and ground goes sodden underfoot.

Even the children start to turn,
their small tight fists becoming shovels
that can dig and dig.

My wife has changed her name again,
the letters on her skin,
as black-limbed hills begin to feed,
their long roots sucking.

There is just no end to what goes on.

5. MAY

Familiar tropings of a Spring Abstract:
the apple trees in bloom,
the house in gold, glad-handing light,
the garden path now fraught with bees.

Enough of that.
I put my face into the grass and breathe.
I root among the stones
and feel the singe of my own brightness,
light from light,
a speechless passage through a shimmer-time.

• • •

My project for the sun is more than words.
It involves this house,
now blazing whitely on the hill of noon.
It involves the bumblebee
that works its way from bloom to bloom.
It involves an urge to lift myself
beyond this frame,
beyond the difference of word and thing,
this pale Abstract,
the hackneyed rhythms we were born to sing
in Mary's month, dum-derry-derry-ding.

6. JUNE

The house is in a flush of expectation.

For the uncut grass,
which deepens into noon.

For tiny swallows bunched in eaves
or dipping through the dusk.

For the pond that rises, fed invisibly
from streams below, its fringe of weeds
lashed to and fro.

And for the children:
long legs running on the minty world,
immaculate before their fall to mud,
their graceless tumble
on the trek to home.

7. JULY

Here is the spark of heaven,
rising on the Fourth, the spangled night
of firefall flakes, the glitzy stars.

I let the pond uphold my spirits,
drunk with day's long exaltations,
floating on a raft of fellow-feeling
as the children swarm in rings around me
and the rockets spray.

The universe expands to fill my chest,
an outward crackle, ribs uncaged,
my bird-heart flown to God-knows-where.

The birth of freedom is my theme tonight,
the crack of rifles,
no more King, no taxes from abroad,
and each hand counts.

We'll tax ourselves from here on out.
We'll make ourselves the only kings.
We'll feed the people on the bread of truth.
We'll raise the children to believe for sure
that every color is divinely lit,
that every stone is God's own flint,
that free means free
not only here but there as well,
wherever in the world the star-flakes fall,
the moon is swelling,
and the ponds fill up and go on filling.

I climb the stairwell into light again,
a kitchen lit by lemons in a bowl,
by late November's pooling light.

The children will be waking soon,
but I have time to squeeze the oranges
and pour the milk, remembering
the way my father rose without a clock,
and always in the dark. He'd stoke
the fire with chunks of coal,
then lay our boots out, pair by pair,
and stir the porridge over glass-blue flame.

These daily turns are what sustain me
through the passing days
as I ascend the spiral of each season,
reaching upward to the rosy light,
the only sun that can sustain me
in the world above,
beyond this rude vernacular that plays
for time, this temporizing phase,
beyond this circle of repeating days.

12. DECEMBER

The children have all left.
Their beds are empty, and the drawers hang out.
The bowls and spoons no longer chatter.

I have read the books along that shelf
beside that window.

8. AUGUST

Bounty, bounty.

And the children multiply and feed
like loaves and fishes.
And the crickets thrum in weedy corners
but are not a plague.
The corn is high above our heads
and spilling into ears, so ripe and sweet.
The garden tumbles with its plenty:
beans, potatoes, peppers, kale.

Improbably
we sit and talk of cities
where the streets are hard,
the sidewalks slept on by a thousand souls
in coinless, dreamless, lamplit wonder.
We condemn the nights where crack is king,
where guts are shredded for the smallest change,
where Programs fail,
where death has lost the power of troping.

Nothing in the world outside this text,
I want to say.
I want this text to hold, to cover
bodies on the street.
I want it for a net to catch what falls.
I want it, like a spider's web, to shake
when any strand, oh anywhere, is touched.

9. SEPTEMBER

I saw it through a net of rain at dusk:
the field in fall,
its tearlike traceries against the pane.

The stones were sponges
left outside all night to drink,
the grass was sopping.
Leaves cut loose and flattened on the mud.

I could almost not believe the world
beyond those fields:
the God-abandoned gullies, cliffs of fear,
the deadhead swamps,
streams disappearing into deeper woods.

I put a log on,
watched it waken into flame.
I felt the warmth, the hiss to crackle,
fall to fire,
while somewhere overhead
the black geese flew, V after V,
a honking wedge of autumn knowledge
I would never have.

Their south was simile to me, no more;
their teleology was not my own.
I was here, and winterbound, and staying—
though the leaves went brown and visions failed
in traceries, in tears.

10. OCTOBER

Leafmeal, gild: the glory of a wood
too deep in dying to rehearse old times.
The tinsel days are full of flutter,
an advancing wind like military drums
before the slaughter of a billion lives.
We've come to die, but nobody complains
as bannerols are flown, as flags go snap.
The General is waving from his hill,
is mounted on his high, white horse of clouds.
There's rock and drill, a draft of courage,
bugles like we've never heard before.
The death of dying is the only death
that matters, but it's not within
our purview now; this loud, full battle
has our eyes, our ears in thrall;
we're ankle-deep in all these corpses,
mulch and mangle, in the fell of fall.

11. NOVEMBER

The cellarhole is filled with dark,
the smell of apples rotting in a bin,
the stench of clay.
I sweep my hand through cobwebs streaming
from the joists and rafters
to adjust the settings on the furnace.
Old pipes hiss.

• • •

Each of them is full of marginalia
I cannot decipher.
They will never help me through this day,
old books like friends too long abandoned.
It is not their fault that time must come.

A fire burns low, mid-afternoon;
the last log jolts to crumble in the grate,
with ashes on my tongue.

In winter woods, the fox is sleeping,
As I walk the fields to see if I can find
what can't be found.

You're not there standing in the husks of corn.
You're not there floating in the black pond water.
Not a whisper in the whitest limbs,
the beautiful appalling grove of trees.

So late to question, but I must insist.

Who knows what happens to the little seeds
that fail to prosper?
Who knows if what is taken by the wind
will ever be returned?

III

The Ruined House

THE LOST SCENT

Winds off the dumps bring back a childhood
gone, long gone:
the reek of acid-tinged mine water,
smolder of the culm in lowly humps
beside the graveyard
where my father's fathers drift in seams.

I've tried to lose so many things,
too many things,
and now this wind refuses to die down;
it carries in its multiple, gray folds
these whiffs and gleanings
from another life, once all my own.

1954

Warm rain in winter,
and for days the streets
were all awash
in downtown Scranton,
gray snow melting,
sewers overwhelmed.
I went to school without
a hat, without
a thought of what
might follow: flood
or fright, unnatural
disasters. Hours
into dusk I drummed
my fingers on the desk
at school as windows
darkened and the glass
was streaked. My teacher
wept, I don't know why.
I found my mother crying
in the kitchen. I do not
know why. Sometimes
the waters must give way,
the skies tear open,
barrels overflow
and gutters run.

SAYERS LEDGE

I took a low path, turning
at the Church of St. Theresa, cutting
through the patch, its iron weeds
and dandelion dust.

The footbridge held me
just above the stream,
its skin tatooed with cables,
and the moon a splotch of cream.

The crickets thrummed in brush,
and down the valley I could hear
the boxcars clicking, coupling
in the August dusk.

I cocked an ear,
kept to the path behind
the dump, whose red-blue smolder
was a wound I wore, but older.

It was not all mine,
the stain that spread across the county,
only partly mine. I found the trail
behind the breaker and began

the climb toward a view, that point
of purchase overlooking all:

the long blue valley coiling
on itself, its voice unheard

beyond these shouldering black hills.
I found my place on Sayers Ledge
and sat there. I was still
above it, climbing

in a smoke-drift, valley rue,
still straining, even choked. I knew
enough to feel a little angry,
not enough to think it through.

KEYSER VALLEY: 1963

A string of blue lights, burning
into dusk; the used cars
huddle, fading as they shine,
a river of debris illumined
by its glower, a wash of dreams.
Some kid in jeans slicks
back his forelock, listens
to a tune: "Love, only love"—
his Chevy plowing
through the tall imagined grain
of what he wants:
the loose-hipped women
he has seen in books, their eyes
like fishhooks, nails
of horn. He slips
through gears, the motions
of his blood, teeth clenched
or grinding. Junkyards
glimmer from the roadway banks,
spare parts, accessories,
a blush of chrome,
bright universal joints,
wire wheels and mirrors.
"Love me every day,"
the hot wind's singing,
"Love me every night."
His engine throttles. Moonlight
drapes the valley with its gown.

TO MY FATHER IN LATE SEPTEMBER

A cold sky presses at my window,
and the leaves at every edge go brown.
I watch and listen,
though the walls are thick between us now.
The apples on the tree inside the garden
fall, unpicked. I let them fall
as I must fall and you, my father,
too must fall and sooner
than I'm willing yet to grant.
These blunt successions still appall me:
father into son to dying son,
the crude afflictions of a turning world
that still knows nothing and will never
feel a thing itself, this rock
that's drilled and blasted, cultivated,
left to dry or burn. We soon must learn
its facelessness in sorrow,
learn to touch and turn away,
to settle in the walls of our composure
and assume a kind of winter knowledge,
wise beyond mere generation
or the ruthless overkill of spring.

THE CROW-MOTHER
TELLS ALL

The empty oil drums rattled in the yard
that day in Scranton, and the ham-red hills
would shudder in the distance, thunder-chilled.
My mother shucked a dozen ears of corn,
feeding me stories of the swoop and killings
I could say by heart and still can say.
She hovered in the dust-light, railed
as porch lamps flickered and the power failed,
but not in her. The boom-and-tingle of the storm
was half by her imagined. Hanging on the hard
wings of her apron, always in her sway,
I listened as the green ears all were torn,
her face by lightning cracked and clawed,
her laughter tumbling, beaked and cawed.

GRANDMOTHERS

I. RUTH ANN CLIFFORD (1898–1964)

Fat girl, folded in an ignorance
not bliss, she waded into fields in central
Pennsylvania, wishing she could fly.

No flight was possible, of course, for her.
She was seventeen, and too-soon-gravid.
"Lift up your eyes unto the hills,"
her mother quoted from the only Book
she'd ever seen. The far, blue hills
were all she had now, waiting for his child.

He'd come, not courting, from another county,
crossed her borders, lost himself
in uplands, rolling country. She would later
tell us "he was never mean."

The words came slow to her thick tongue.
Her poverty was silence well-maintained
through empty decades, folded hands;
she prayed for something like release
those August evenings in West Scranton,
with her daughters mewling in their rooms like cats,
her husband leaning over rails and spitting,
and the hills a little closer every year.

II. IDA PARINI (1890–1976)

A drowning was the one thing she remembered
from the other side,
how the roiling sea gave up a girl
one morning on the beach
in old Liguria, where she was born.

The body was like alabaster, cool;
the hair was dandled by the lurid waters,
to and fro. She'd known the girl
"not very well."

              If pressed, she'd say
Liguria was full of shaggy rats; her father
shot them with a long-nosed pistol.
It was not so hard to leave all this.

The crossing she remembered wave by wave.
The maggoty old meat, the swampy water,
how her cousin died of fever
on the mid-Atlantic,
though she suffered "less than one might think."

Her parents left her lonely at the docks
with someone twice her age or more.
He had golden cuff-links, ivory teeth.
They married in Manhattan
as her parents sailed to Argentina,
where an earthquake swallowed their last days.
"It was not as if I really knew them."

She was left alone in Pennsylvania
with her five small sons.
She did not complain, though once or twice
I found her sitting by the swollen river
near her house, her long hair down.
When I would ask her what was wrong
she would say she'd lost so many people
she had scarcely known.
It was "not as bad as I imagined,
but you sometimes wonder what was meant."

SUNDAY DRIVES IN
PENNSYLVANIA

Our red-finned '57 Chevy nosed upstream,
a prehistoric fish in no real element
except nostalgia for a future life
of fins and leather, chromium and steel.
With Daddy in the front beside our mother,
we were that hard nut: a nuclear
and self-borne unit on the road
to Better Things. My sister sat beside me
in the back on vinyl cushions, ready
as we lit out once again for open country,
the imagined pines, tall standing corn,
macadam roads that licked their tongues
in small, dark corners where the mossbanks grew
and mothwebs gathered in the toes of trees.

Daddy would drive slow, too slow
for sassy, souped-up kids in street rods
going nowhere at their chosen speed,
whose only hope was but to dazzle
in their prime, just once before the fall,
when life went downhill fast forever
into bells and Zip-waxed winding halls,
the corridors of powerless, pure boredom
where they'd have to live and work for decades
till The End was scrolled on little screens,
soon followed by some static and white fuzz.
• • •

We took off after church, our good clothes
hung on racks again, in shorts and sport shirts,
leaving Scranton as one leaves one's memory
on hold and ventures forth into the future,
half pretending one might not go back.
We motored on, past cemeteries, churches,
tenements, and crumbling stucco buildings
where the V.F.W. and Legion met
to mourn the past that's never present
in the minds of youths who've not known war
or real destruction. On the painted steps
of wood-frame homes, young married men
wore crisp white T-shirts and would nurse
long beers all afternoon, their radios
tuned in to Connie Mack or Yankee Stadium,
their young wives herding loudmouthed gangs
through hot backyards to public pools
where ear infections were believed to breed.
Good-bye, we waved. Good-bye, good-bye.

We passed the railyards and the slaggy dumps,
the warehouse rows, the giant bakery
with broken windows and the darkened mills
where bombs were made through World War II,
working our way to breezy suburbs
where the newly solvent middle classes
had begun to learn to lose their souls,
past new split-levels that we all adored,
the sprinklers whirring in concentric rings
around the silent, sunny-seeming lives
that Daddy guarded with his life insurance.
My mother was afraid of them, refusing

to allow herself to meet their gaze.
We drove on by. "One day you'll live
in neighborhoods like this one," Daddy said,
now tightening the grip on his red wheel.
We could feel the pistons pull us free
of civilized, suburban-bred contentment
as we lunged toward a wilder country
where the brooks ran white in fizzy rapids
and the killdeer dipped their beaks in ponds
and huckleberries fed a thousand bears.
The sunlight poured profusely on a land
that answered back with undiluted green.

Now when I'm weary of what has become
of worlds at hand, considering the way
that even wilderness cannot be found
on far-off, undiscovered ground,
I hope to find it somewhere in myself,
remembering those lazy Sunday drives
to somewhere one could only half believe:
the blurry velvet of the uncut fields,
great copper beeches in the middle distance
and, beyond, blue hills and bluer sky.

THE SMALL ONES LEAVE US

The small ones leave us, and the leaves are blown.
It doesn't matter what we do or say,
there's nothing in the end that we can own.

The facts, of course, are all well-known.
We should have understood that come what may
the small ones leave us, and the leaves are blown.

There's nothing in the world that's not on loan:
young children, trees, this house of days.
There's nothing in the end that we can own.

So why regret that each of them has grown?
Why grieve when grasses turn to hay?
The small ones leave us, and the leaves are blown.

This accidental harvest has been sown
and willy-nilly reaped in its own way.
There's nothing in the end that we can own.

What little we can make of skin and bone
unsettles us, who watch and sometimes pray
as small ones leave us and the leaves are blown.
There's nothing in the end that we can own.

NEW MORNING

Light seeps through chinks
as sparrows in the leaves
break out in chatter. Breezes
shift the gauzy curtains,
slip along the wall:
the chill blue fingers
of a northern spring. I let
the blinds up, watching
features I have come to love
spread out before me
like a brassy sea.
I cup your breasts,
the slow warmth of your body
lengthened to my own.
I float upon the surf, the rising
swell of our affection,
driven to the shores
of what we need. Outside,
the world begins without us,
traffic through the lights,
the early news at six o'clock.
The copper river coils
in the sun. It's time, you say,
that you must go.
Reluctantly, at last,
I let you go, loosen my grip,
let all my kisses turn to air
and lie here by myself

a further hour, thinking
of the way this world
collects us even from ourselves.
My friend, dear bright
incendiary skin,
tomorrow we must love
beyond these boundaries
of day and night,
of wax and wane,
must go on loving even
like the hills that break
beyond New Hampshire into Maine.

ADRIFT

As night glooms over, slowly
in the bed we rock to sleep,
unmoored, a craft dislodged,
riding the ripples out to sea.
Rain ticks the windows, roof
and walls, a misty drizzle.
Fog comes down
and hovers in the wood
like thinking without words.
We lean into the unspecific
dark, exhausted by the
to-and-fro of accusation.
You said one thing and I
another: neither of us lied,
but language is a wide net cast
at random in the sharpest seas.
The quiver of our catch
is still. We drift now,
tongueless, listing as the rain
sleeks down our house, as
blear November nuzzles us
asleep. We sleep to dream,
we dream to meet the images
that tell and tell again,
to waken into clarity
and names, the speech that
binds us, brings us safely
into dry dock, dawn.

DEMONIAL

They rustle toward you in the dark,
their legions cutting through a mountain trace,
nosing upstream along a bank,
or filing through a basin like red ants,
aware that patience is the way to luck,
the only way to find you in the end.

You can't dissuade them, so give in:
put out some milk or water in a bowl,
a tantalizing morsel that will give them pause.

Pull up a chair, rehearse your speech.
It doesn't matter if, at last, you fail
to ward them off: it's how you greet them,
smiling or with frozen lips and jaw,
your eyes like lightning or a low-watt bulb.

HOUSE ON FIRE

My house on fire in the midday sun
is more than I can watch.
My kindling sons, their fragile bodies,
turn to light.
My wife is lost in auguries of rain.
I take her hand, it turns to wind.
Dry grass is blazing on a windy knob
just out of sight,
as rats take cover in the distant barns.
The woodchucks dig.
The sheep and rocks are huddling in the fields.
My books are curling in the fiery tongues
that want this babble,
that would eat a house so finely cobbled
stone by stone, my house of paper,
flesh and words,
so easily become this fly-ash, bonemeal,
dust of language sucked and blown.

THE RUINED HOUSE

Deep in the woods, beyond the shuffle
of our works and days, we found a path
between an alley of Norwegian pines.
The children ran on spongy needles,
disappearing in the purple shade;
their shouts were lost among the bird-yip:
tremolo of wood-doves, long diphthong
of redwing blackbirds, crass old crows
all harping on the same old note again.
Your hand in mine, we seemed to drift upon
a fuzzy cumulous of half-voiced thoughts:
the tongue's quick shuttle through the loom of mind
in search of texture, text to sing,
recitativo of a thousand glimpses
caught, composed. All along the way
the eye sought gleanings, images to tell,
to cast one's thoughts on, fix the swell
of meaning in the cross-haired sights
of metaphor, a trope to end all troping:
words and things in pure performance.

Now the hilly path went straightaway ahead,
unfolding with the ease of morning vision.
As they would, the children found it first:
the ruined house on what was once
a breezy hillock in an open field.
The coarse foundation might have been
a dry stone wall like other walls

now winding over hills, down dingly dells,
to parse the complex sentence of our past,
delineating fields no longer found,
obscured by popple, tamarack and vetch.
The stone foundation of the house in ruins
wasn't stern or morally suggestive.
It had just withstood what it could stand—
the falling stars, the tumbledown of snow,
sharp dislocations of the frosty ground,
the weight of timber soaking in the rain.

We stepped inside behind the children,
who were walking beams like tightrope wires
across a corridor that once led somewhere
warm, familial, and full of light.
The cellarhole was still a hutch of night:
one saw it through the intermittent floorboards
and the two-by-fours exposed like vertebrae
that once held everything in place
but powdered now and sagged toward the middle
as the woodmites fed and moisture softened
grainy fibers, as the mulch of days
began in earnest. There was still a roof
aloft amid the trees, a fragile shade
with patches that were open into sky.
The children clambered up a tilting stairwell
to the second floor; we followed suit,
though not so fearlessly and free
of old conceptions—hurtful images
that hold one back, making one wish
for something less or something more.

   •   •   •

The little bedrooms that we found upstairs
were still intact, with built-in beds,
coarse empty shelves still half considering
the weight of objects from their rumored past.
If one stood still and listened close
the voices of the children could be heard,
their laughter in the leaves, the sass and chatter.
Anyway, that's what I told the children,
who believed and listened and could hear.
It's not so hard to frame the past
upon the present, to connect the dots
all still in place, to resurrect and ride
ancestral voices: there is one great tongue.
We find ourselves alive in that old mouth,
through which all meaning flows to sea.
We pour and pour the water of our lives,
a glittery cascade, its brightness falling
into pools where it must darken once again,
must soak in soil, collect and gather
in a place to tap for future soundings.

Later, in the shade behind the house,
we lingered in the garden's dense enclosure.
Petalfall of spring was planted there,
the hard ground turned, the weeds uprooted.
Beans and flowers were assigned to rows.
While he would ditch the upper pasture,
she was left alone sometimes in summer
and would sit there safely in the chestnut shade
to read the Brownings, he and she,
as children napped or slaughtered dragons
with their makeshift swords. That's how the idyll

runs, of course. The typhus and the cold
that cracked the windowpanes in mid-November
and the bitter words: these, too, were true.

We left on hushing feet like thieves
with something in our pockets, awed and fragile.
It was only time that turned those pages,
leaving dust in sunlight on the stairs,
disfiguring the walls that once would keep
a family aloft through hazy fall
and hardy winter into sopping spring.
It was only time that would not stop,
that bore us homeward on the needle path
toward the end of what was ours
a while that summer in the leafy woods.

IV

Another Kingdom

STREET BOYS

Pasolini fished among their schools.
He'd kiss their ears
and whisper challenges and put
his hand in their tight pockets
and go down to depths
from which a chosen few return.

They took his money as they took him in.
He didn't care, but rode
the lilting undertow of dreams
he thought they shared. It was not to flatter
when he called them brave,
lapping their shores, the hard blue rocks
on which he crashed.

A CONVERSATION IN OXFORD

for Isaiah Berlin

Euphonious if not in sync the bells
beat time in amber chapel towers,
and the time has come for tea and talk.
We settle in a room of many shades,
the questions you have spent the decades turning.

"What can we assume about this world?"
you wonder, once again. "What can we claim?"
So little, it would seem. The weak foundations
of all human knowledge make one shudder
to assume too much, to claim too boldly.

"What do you believe?" you ask, so frankly
that I redden, turn, avert my eyes.
"Is consciousness itself an end or foretaste
of a fuller life? This 'oversoul' that Emerson
proposed: Whatever does it mean?"

The honeying facades along the High Street
seem impervious to dwindling light;
whole generations are absorbed
in rheumy passages and darkened cloisters
where so many questions have been put

and left unanswered. It was not a failure
not to answer. I assume that you,
over the decades, have refused to grant

those easy answers that can dull a heart,
occlude a mind, can chain a soul.

You tap your pipe and offer this:
"Real liberty is found in fine gradations,
dartings of the mind—not Big Ideas,
which are mostly preludes to deceit,
embodiments of someone's will-to-power."

I scan the rows of volumes you have filled
with annotations in the well-kept nights—
from Plato to Descartes, from Kant to Kripke.
Herzen was a friend, and Vico, too.
You say that all the best books seize us

half by chance, interrogate and turn us
loose upon ourselves again. I mostly listen,
letting what you say fill up the hour.
The room grows violet and dusky,
insubstantial, as your voice compels

and seems to quicken as your flesh dissolves.
And soon the darkness is itself complete,
consuming everything except your language,
which assumes an Old World gaiety and calm.
I feel, myself, an apparition.

"It is strange," I say. "We find ourselves
alive without a reason, inarticulate
but always trying to re-form a thought
in words that never seem quite right."
I see a flicker in your candle-eyes.

•   •   •

"The world is what it is," you answer strictly,
having seen enough of it to say.
"The world is what you claim it is
as well: this dwindling light, the smoke
of reason, ghostly words in ghostly air."

I claim this hour, a plum-deep dusk,
the need to pose so many questions,
late, so late—an Oxford afternoon
when everything but language falls away
and words seem all the world we need.

ANOTHER KINGDOM

In memory of Marion Shonstrom

There is another kingdom under dirt,
a world within the world we touch and taste,
as bright and bitter
as a plum that's mouthed to sudden bursting.

They will all say no,
that dirt is dirt and dust is dust;
a rock that falls and breaks upon itself
is many pebbles,
each of them discrete and hard and void.
They will say this bravely, wisely, gravely.

I will say that once in Scotland in the spring
I found a patch of bluebells in the woods.
When I bent to touch them,
I was there and nowhere.
I was then and now.

There is another kingdom under dirt.
When night falls over us
at last, forever, may we start
from somewhere that to narrow eyes
looks like an ending,
even as the wind takes its beginning
from the stillest air.

AMALFI DUSK

The sun's a red kite caught in branches,
and the town's aflame.
A ruby sea nibbles its fingers,
curls its tail into a limestone cliff;
the hillside flickers with the fire of stones,
late winter lemons hung like globes.
Goats and children chase the light
through close and cloister.
Wrists of smoke are reaching for the sky.

In consecrated soil above the town,
the fathers linger,
making infinite bright circles
in the mind of God,
beyond the pain of composition
as we know it here,
words calling out to words
for something finer,
something we can sing or say aloud,
a cadence we cannot unlearn.

The dead are lucky.
It is those with matter left to burn
who wish for more,
who need the madder rose of dusk,
the bank of kindling,
matchtips, candles, kisses, tears.

GOOD FRIDAY IN AMALFI

The terrace is a tier of flame tonight,
a lavish send-off to the day,

the red sea curling in the stony cove,
the town lights flickering, a mass of candles

on the dusky shore. Good-bye, I wave,
as long-limbed vines begin to chitter

and the rose-thorns dig, their chafers glinting.
Arum lilies blow their hornlike buds.

Behind my house, the bare-faced cliff
maintains a solitary crooked grin

as if it knows what I have done
or left undone, my desultory sins.

But now it's over, I pretend, near dark,
lifting my arms in racy wind—

white wind that fits me like a loose soutane.
The moon's a wafer dipped in blood.

Signore, I could leave it all tonight.
I could rise—all flutter, whip, and burn.

STILL LIFE

Late afternoon, somewhere in England
by a bowl of apples just past peak,
I could see again: there are no ordinary objects.
Each is lovely in its odd one-offness,
which implies an origin
as strange as mine or yours.
And each is dying in its slow-burn way,
a decomposing that repeats the fall:
a kind of withering bronze sadness
as the skins go dark in different places,
soft and mottled like a baby's scalp,
the fontanel depressed. I could understand
their near disguise in clubby sameness,
and the need to pause in waning sunlight
in a milky bowl. They seek
an equilibrium, a fictive moment
where they feign a freedom from decay
or boring growth. I feel that way
sometimes but lack their classical repose,
the waxy sheen that coddles brightness but allows
a casual release of light,
that sense of safety in small numbers
gathered in a haze, in ripeness
general beyond each shrinking globe,
a fragrance that assembles slowly in the air,
that enters air as fruity emanation,
filling up the room with life, still life.

MAREOTIS

An Essay on Mind

The Witch of Atlas flew above the Nile
beyond the Nile to that still center
where a mirror-lake reveals all things:
whatever happened, what did not,
what is, and what we take to be.
The moving pictures flashed before her:
myriad of pumped-up, primal images
that lacked for nothing but embodiment
in words—a text to memorize and say.

Plotinus theorized but never saw
bright Mareotis, legendary lake
where cocks might crow on pebbled banks
without a sound, where music is unformed
but drifts like mist through woody patches
and where sunflowers turn their faces
upward to an ice-blue empty sky
reflecting everything that lives below it,
imitatio without recension,
color-perfect to the nth degree:
the zero noon of correspondent dreaming
wherein sky and water shine as one
in shadowless perfection.

Mind as mirror.

It's just the same old metaphor rehashed
through toppling ages, but we can't resist

this invitation to a final trope,
a metaphor collapsing on itself
as world and word fold in together
in a timeless flash beyond this tracing
in a measured scrawl, this poetry
of wistful lunging toward, this seeking after
what's been sensed or partially revealed
in flints of language, shards of thought
that draw us down to that lost stream
the Witch of Atlas followed to its source.
She found, not nature, but *la bella natura*,
idealized beyond the poor reflection
we encounter daily as we try to think
and speak and write, so cruelly aware
of that wide fissure every subject feels
in confrontation with the object-world,
whose countenance conceals a frown or, worse,
a sneering glance redoubled in the mirror.

Mirror mirror.

       Sadness often fills us
as we scan the world and hope to find,
Narcissus-like, a face that we may own.
There's nothing there, we soon discover,
and we walk away, perhaps a little miffed.
The self needs replication to survive:
an image it can hold, some Mareotic
surface that gives back at least as much
as what is given.

  • • •

Once upon a time
I went out walking with my son in woods
in late September, and we found a lake
half hidden in a ring of fiery trees.
The boy was taken by its perfect sheen:
"The lake keeps thinking of those trees,"
he said. I could hear a yearning in that voice
that I still hear, though he is older now
and won't remember how the maples lost
their leaves around us, how the poplars bled
into the water as the too-still lake
kept thinking of those trees, kept taking them
to heart.

The Witch of Atlas
sat upon the mossbank, peering into space
and listening for a clue, perhaps an answer.
But there are no answers, only images
and sleights of language that reveal
a little less than satisfies our thirst
for something more. If only we could look
as closely as she did, we too might see
the mirror's tain, which holds and helps
the image to sustain its shimmering facade;
we too might see, beneath the gleam,
that shadow underneath the water's
water, depths where even fish are blind,
where emptiness is ripened into all.

NEAR PITLOCHRY

As the sun cut through a cloud,
the hills lit up
like bulbs switched on by unseen hands;
the wind began its spiral climb
from hutch to valley
to the saw-toothed crags where thistle burns.
Alone, in winter,
with my face toward a frost-lit bush,
I waited and was met.

I WAS THERE

I say it, I was there.
No matter what the yellow wind has taken,
I was there, with you.
We have walked out early in the spring
beside the river, when the sun's red shield
was caught in branches
and the bud-tips bled.
We have plucked ripe berries from a hill of brush
in mid-July,
and watched the days go down in flames
in late September,
when the poplar shook its foil.
We have walked on snow in January light:
the long white fields were adamantly bright.
I say it, I was there.
No matter that the evidence is gone,
we heard the honking of the long black geese
and saw them float beyond the town.
Gone all those birds, loose-wristed leaves,
the snowfire, days
we cupped like water in our hands.
So much has slipped through fragile hands.
The evidence is lost, but not these words.
You have my word:
I say it, I was there.

V

*Reading Emerson in
My Forty-seventh Summer*

READING EMERSON IN MY FORTY-SEVENTH SUMMER

1 .

The eye is the first circle, Emerson once said.
And so I gather what the world can give
by taste and smell, by touch and ear,
but mostly through the faculty of vision,
the observing eye, *whose innocent
attachment to all passing things is always
sudden, rapt, and pure.* I see, I am.
The eye, percipient, becomes the I.

Beginning with the eye: the strict observance
of what is is difficult; *the mind
unfocused sees too much to see at all.*
I must learn to sit beside this pond
above the cattails, on the mossy bank,
and to study green, concentric circles
widening like rings around a stone
from that still center that we call the self.

And what I see can multiply my sight
beyond what object I may hold in view:
*the flutter of a swallow's tail in flight
becomes a sweet correlative at dusk
beside the pond.* It comes from nowhere,
swoops and zooms, like any other thought
in vivid flight from pure abstraction,
lives a moment and is real, then gone.

• • •

I would see the world's ten thousand things:
unlettered, nameless, larruping and lewd,
the full account before me always,
and the eye's horizon open to regard
the endless catalogue of high and low,
the skimming swallow and the world it sweeps
behind it as it dips and veers beyond
its rippling shadow in the dusky pond.

2 .

Our life, he said, *is an apprenticeship.*
There is no end. No end in nature, none.
And every end is a beginning. *There is no*
conclusion. I must not conclude.
Under every deep a lower deep
is waiting to be found. I would understand
more deeply if I could, and I must try.

Thus far, I've often been mistaken,
having lived perhaps too much for bygones,
things long spent. Each child has hurt me
with its urgent will-to-break the mold,
each shoe irrelevant in X of days,
each toy absurd in twenty minutes.
I have tried like ancient Chinese mothers
to restrict their feet, to bind their wills.
I have tried to keep the world the same
day after day, to worship noon and hate
the avalanche of time that darkens
and occludes what once seemed bright.
I have kept my recipes the same:
lunch every day of toast and tuna,

coffee with a little milk and sugar.
It is pure nostalgia. Yet my friends
keep changing, or their diets do.
My house grows darker year by year,
or so it seems on sultry days
when every thought is heavy, as if rain
had soaked cerebral membranes
and the very notion of another day
is pain itself, the prospect of decay.

I must learn to live as Emerson
in Concord learned to live, *a celebrant
of change, unstable of conviction*,
set on nothing but what isn't fixed,
aware that ends are only means,
that even if I lose a past I loved—
my mother in her apron cooking dinner,
father in his paint-stained, weekend jeans—
it's still a part of some large pattern,
that the dead are with us, everywhere at once,
and what has gone will come again.
The wheel must turn upon itself,
the spokes must fly; *the axle is the eye
that penetrates the whir and whirl,
the circular of days that spins around
with no beginning, and without an end*.

No theologian, Emerson could see
that churches never house a living God.
God lives *in orchards, ancient trees,
in rocks and rills*. And so he set out daily
on his walks beyond the town. Communion

was the goal of each excursion,
and these walks became a firm foundation
for the church he built of vaulting words.
A man should live by walking lightly
in the world-at-large, the breaking days
like wafers on his tongue, his head upright.
A man should learn to live in time,
which plays the host and entertains him
for a little while, then leaves him free
to wander in the aisles of ancient trees
beyond the circus of his tumbling days.

3 .

The metamorphosis of nature shows
itself no more than this; that there
is no word in our language that cannot
become typical to us of nature
by giving it emphasis.

And so
we call the world by different names.
It's like a tapestry hung out in space.
The world's a web, a spider's entrails spun
to catch whatever falls. The world's a text
for exegesis and for emendation:
syntax is the ground we walk upon,
its undulating hills and valley floors
a kind of language we must learn to read.
The world's a fragile craft we steer
through choppy waters; it's a cup, a cave,
a crystal maze, a coffin, or a well
that pours and pours, is infinitely deep
and cool and ready to be drawn.

It's always changing, shifting shapes.
And happiness, he said, *is only in
the moment of transition: spark to spark,*
the leap between two poles, the synapse bridged,
however briefly in the long, dull night
without connection, metaphor, or trope.

4 .
All things unfix, dispart, and flee.
He might have written that to me.
I've seen it happening: the unhinged door,
a well run dry, my foot gone sore.
I've seen my father strain to bend,
my mother, too. No god can mend
the human animal beyond a point;
the doctor may prevent a swollen joint,
may kill bacteria that flood the heart,
put off by years the moment to depart,
but things unfix, dispart, and flee.
I know this as I know what I can see.

5 .
There is something in life untranslatable.
It cannot be said and won't be said.
It will not be carried over into speech,
and yet, without it, there could be no speech.
*Like bars of gold in some dark vault
it gives our money powers of exchange.*
Our words are tender that we learn to spend;
their currency is based on what we know
but cannot say, on what we guess at,
sometimes hint at, darkly over drinks.
Its counterfeit is everywhere but worthless:

we have all been paid in those thin bills.
No matter. It is safe within that safe,
that vaulted silence which attunes our ears
and beckons us to words like antique coins.

6 .
The heart has sabbaths and its jubilees.

Shabbat, the holy day of watchfulness
and prayer, of waiting on the world.
I stand quite still and look
about me as the blackbirds rise
to high, thin wires, and leaves are loose
wrists turning on a stem, and earth itself,
which carries us to sleep in daily practice,
imitates the round my life must follow.

When we stand quite still, the time is holy,
even when the cars like yellowjackets sting,
when every hand is turning to a task,
when nothing ever really seems to stop:
the heart has sabbaths and its jubilees.

The jubilees are moments out of time,
but timed to rescue us from time.
As when we hear the apples falling
and can understand that all things fall
and not feel sad. Or see the child
changing underfoot, and can rejoice
in subtle changes that must bring it down.
Or taste a sudden kiss at midnight,
and begin to understand our fate

as someone who has loved and, yes, been loved.
What little things can make us weep.
The heart has sabbaths and its jubilees.

7 .

For we are not pans and barrows, nor even
porters of the fire and torchbearers,
but children of the fire, made of it.

The fire in these fingertips is mine, and yours.
I'm match-lit, lucent, flint and fuel:
a blaze of words. Whatever I would touch
must burn as well: the world's my tinder,
and my breath will fan into a bonfire,
flame, flare out. I've seen the rocks
turn molten red, the rivers in their sheets
of fire unquenched.
                    It's just the sun,
a cold white sun, that sets them burning.

We were stones in space, he told us,
frozen out of time. We entered flesh
to sizzle as we do, the soul on fire.
Without this burning there would be no bother,
yes-and-no or do-and-don't. Without it,
I could never walk here, hand in hand,
or put my lips to your white neck.
Without it, I could never see God's face.

We are on our way to whitest ash,
he said. He understood that fire
is transformation, and that smoke is soul

released from body, and that heaven swirls.
For now, let's lick the sky with lightning
and be glad with fire, the long blue flame
that lifts us, lavishes, and lets us burn.

8 .
Other world? There is no other world.

No world but this: the water-blistered rocks
and savvy streams, the fresh-cut grass
and forests with their arms around the wind.
No world but cities like big diamonds
on a cocky finger, and the towns as well,
where shoes are laced and faces scrubbed.
No world but this, its dark sides, too:
the dumps, with sewage leaking into rivers,
slag-heaps, crumbling tenements by parks
where crack is king and guns report
the evening's take, where lowly whispers
find no ears. *No world but this one.*
We must make, remake, and make the world.
This world, the only one we'll have,
is worth remaking, taking for our own.

9 .
The Universe is the externalization of the soul.

A point well-taken, and the only point—
that what we see is also us,
is what we are. For God so loved
this world, the world that we can see:
the red-ripe apples falling through the rain,

the migratory workers who retrieve them,
and the fall itself, its tangy breath
and husks of leaves, the wind that circles
for a place to land, the swirls of grass.
And yet, so much about the fallen world
is hard to love, impossible to take.
I don't love children in the bomb's white eye
or darkness in a mother's face at dusk,
the nil of knowledge she must take to bed;
I don't like poverty within myself,
the lack of sympathy I seem to bear,
must carry like a secret stone till death
grants my forgetting. *It is always hard
to love what fails us, to forgive what fails.*
It's difficult, of course, although I loved it
when I drove my children to their school
through open country, in the morning pink
of light that lay on fresh-cut fields.
This gloria, this mundi. I was glad to tend
the world those days, to do what Emerson
would have us do: *our daily work,
this work of grieving for a fallen world.*

10.
*Work and learn in evil days,
in insulted days, in days of debt,
depression and calamity. Fight best
within the shade of clouds of arrows.*

This sad calamity was God's design;
He botched the world on purpose to prepare
a way, perhaps—the middle way,

a way between the darkness and the dark,
the crude alternatives of good and evil.

Emerson, alone in Concord, understood.
He was not impressed by worldly sinners,
nor would he bow down to starchy saints.
He worked and learned in evil days
and happy ones as well, aware that coins
must always flip, that grimaces and smiles
will tug the same.

        Our first calamity
was birth itself, *that rupture into light*
and fire, fed by darkness. Life
is never won or lost, that much he knew
as moving through the world on brittle grass
he worked and learned in evil days.
He lost so much: a wife and son,
both swallowed at an early age, absorbed
by all the darkness that surrounds us all.

He read so much, forgot so much.
He fought in shadows, under purple clouds
of poisoned arrows, dodging what he could,
but always working, learning what to say
and not to say, aware that silence is a lotus
found and reconstructed, word by word,
that things once heard are never lost,
but saved for songs imagined unto death,
whose end is just a rude beginning
in a world beyond mere right or wrong.

ADM-9680   8/26/98

PS
3566
A65
H68
1997